Aberfoyle, Morriston and Rockton Ontario in Colour Photos, Saving Our History One Photo at a Time

Photography
by Barbara Raué
2014

Series Name:
Cruising Ontario

Book 64: Aberfoyle, Morriston,
Rockton

Cover photo: A Gothic Revival home in Morriston

Series Name: Cruising Ontario
Saving Our History One Photo at a Time

Book 33: Southampton
Book 34: Jarvis
Book 35: Hagersville
Book 36: Caledonia
Book 37: Simcoe
Book 38: Cambridge Part 1 – Galt Book 1
Book 39: Cambridge Part 1 – Galt Book 2
Book 40: Cambridge Part 2 – Preston
Book 41: Cambridge Part 3 – Hespeler
Book 42: Kitchener Book 1
Book 43: Kitchener Book 2
Book 46: Shelburne
Book 47: Alton, Mono and Caledon
Book 48: London in Colour
Book 50: Orangeville Beginnings in Colour
Book 51: Orangeville on Broadway in Colour
Book 52: Orangeville Book 3 in Colour
Book 53: Dundas in Colour Book 1
Book 54: Dundas in Colour Book 2
Book 55: Dundas in Colour Book 3
Book 56: Stratford
Book 57: Hanover
Book 58: New Hamburg Book 1
Book 59: New Hamburg Book 2 and Haysville
Book 60: Waterdown in Colour
Book 61: Burlington in Colour
Book 62: Stoney Creek in Colour
Book 63: Seaforth
Book 64: Aberfoyle, Morriston and Rockton

Other Books by Barbara Raue

Coins of Gold

Arrows, Indians and Love

The Life and Times of Barbara
Volume 1: Inventions That Have Enhanced My Life
Volume 2: Entertainment That I Have Enjoyed
Volume 3: East Coast Trips
Volume 4: Olympics Have Always Intrigued Me
Volume 5: Wonders of the World
Volume 6: Caribbean Cruises We Have Enjoyed
Volume 7: Animals
Volume 8: Storms and Other Major Disasters in My Lifetime
Volume 9: Wars, Terrorist Attacks and Major Disasters

The Cromwell Family Book

Aberfoyle

Puslinch is a township in south-central Ontario in Wellington County south of Guelph. The area is rich in natural gas resources. About half of the township is forested, and a conservation area lies to the southwest. Near the western edge of the township, just outside of Cambridge, Ontario is Puslinch Lake, the largest kettle lake in North America. A kettle lake is a shallow, sediment-filled body of water formed by retreating glaciers or draining floodwaters.

The township includes the communities of Aberfoyle, Aikensville, Arkell, Badenoch, Barbers Beach, Corwhin, Crieff, Killean, Little Lake, Morriston and Puslinch.

Aberfoyle is the administrative centre for Puslinch Township and the municipality's administrative offices and fire station are located here. Aberrfoyle is located at the headwaters of Mill Creek, about ten kilometres south of Guelph. Aberfoyle was first settled in the 1840s and is named for Aberfoyle, Scotland. It is famous for its spring water.

Morriston

Morriston is located in Puslinch Township at Highway 6 and County Road 36, one kilometer south of Highway 401, and sixteen kilometres southeast of Guelph. In 1847 Mr. R. B. Morriston opened a store in one end of his blacksmith shop and two years later built a store on the east side of the road.

Rockton

Rockton is located northwest of Dundas and has been the home of the Rockton's World Fair since 1853.

Table of Contents

Aberfoyle   Page 6

Morriston   Page 9

Rockton   Page 24

Architectural Terms   Page 29

Building Styles   Page 31

Aberfoyle

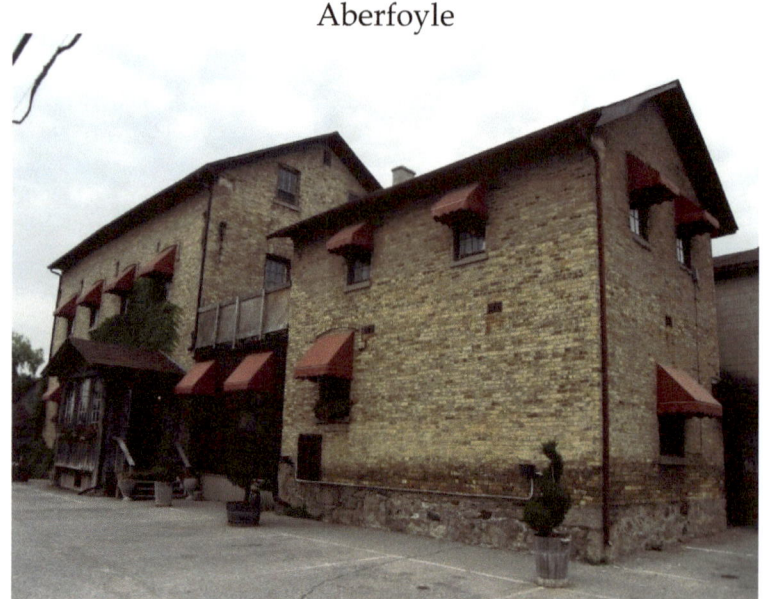

Aberfoyle Mill

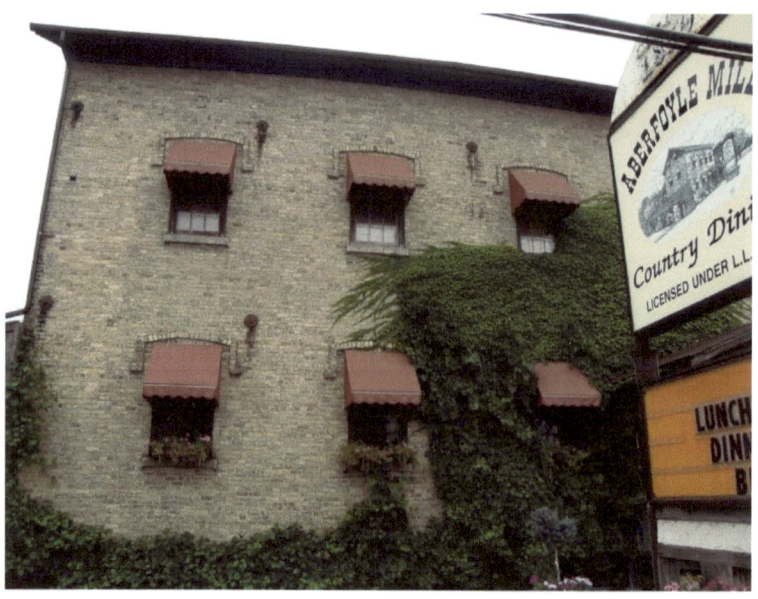

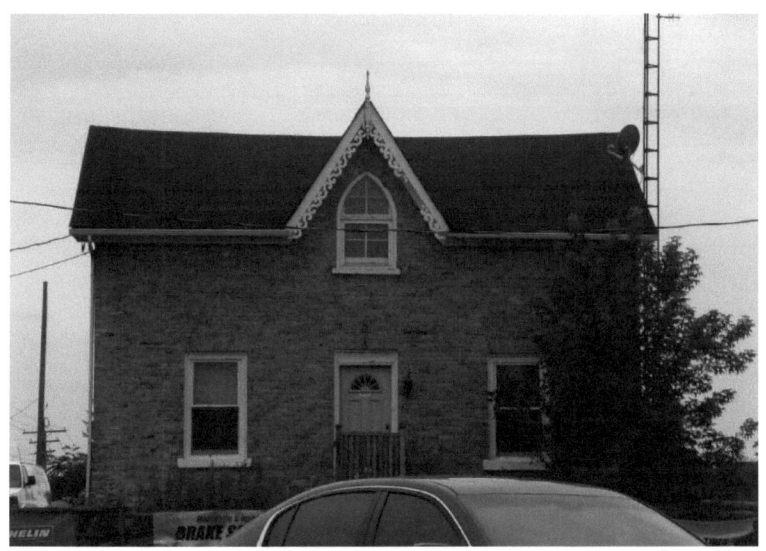

Gothic Revival – verge board trim on gable

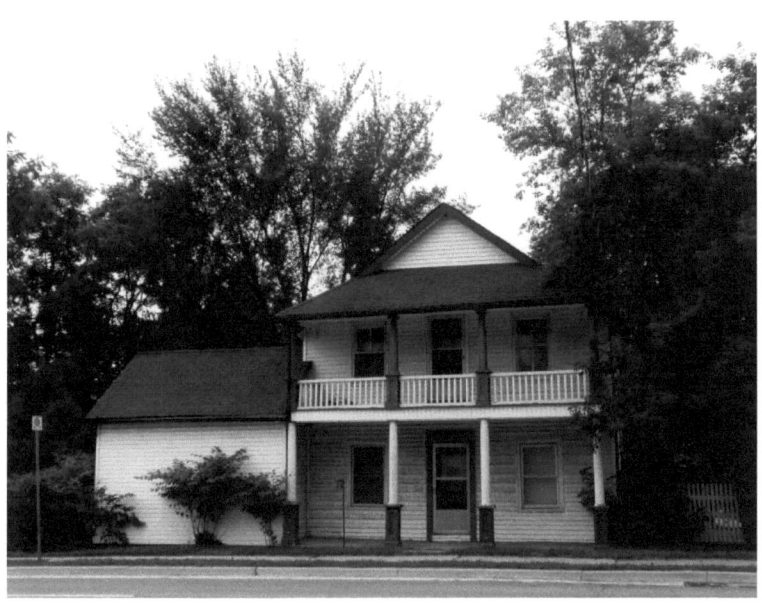

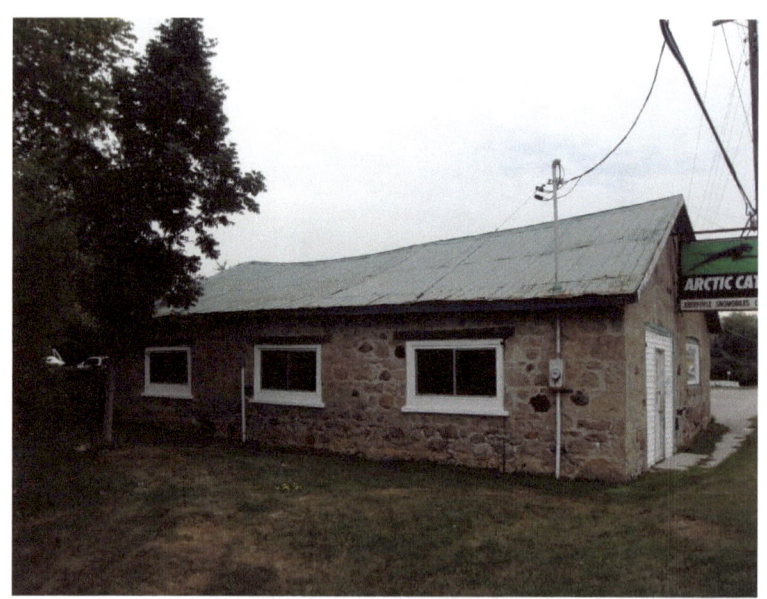

Stone architecture

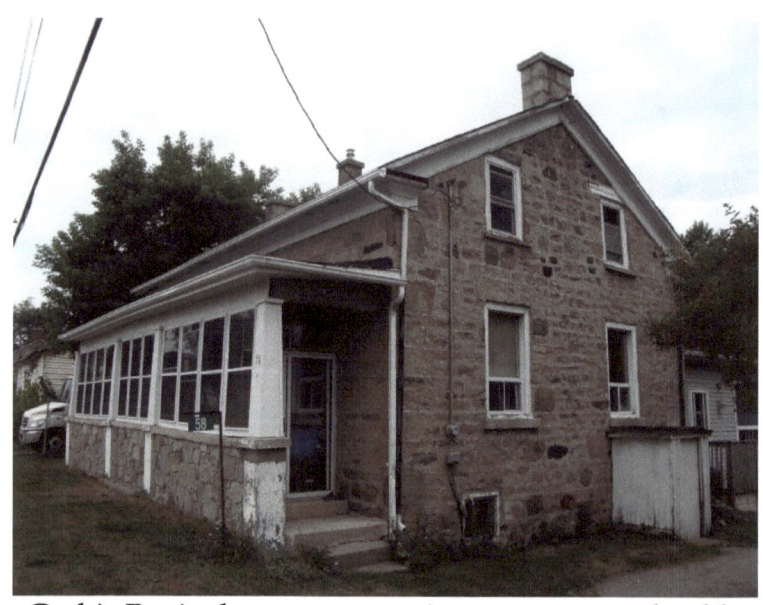

Gothic Revival – stone – cornice return on end gable

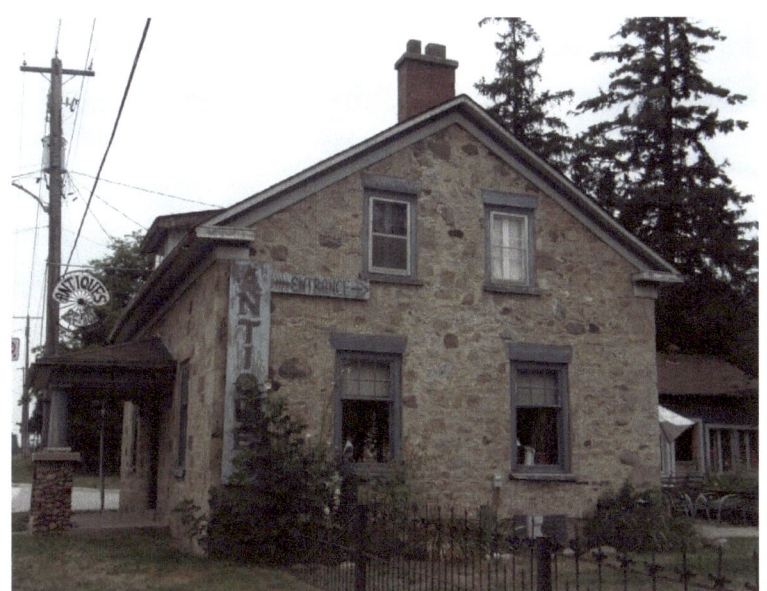

Gothic Revival – stone – cornice return on end gable

Morriston

School Section No. 9 – 1889, Puslinch

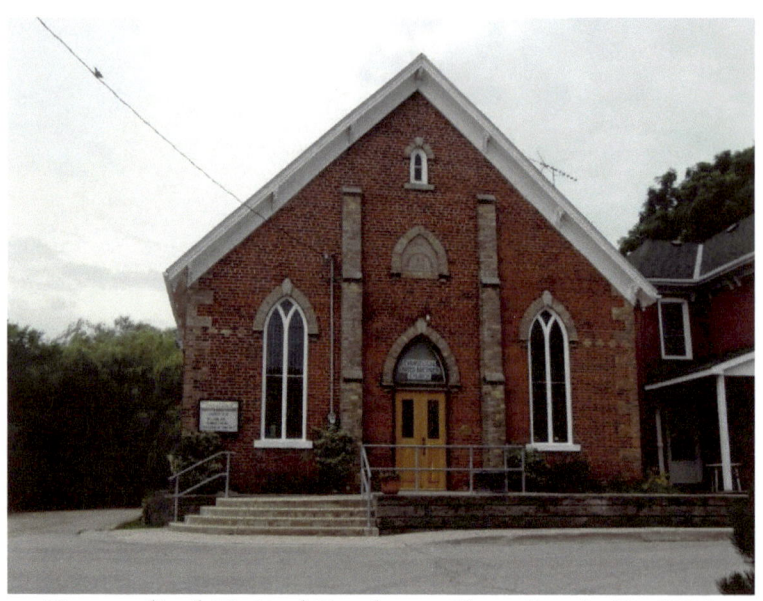

Evangelical United Brethren Church - A. D. 1880
Mount Carmel-Zion United Church

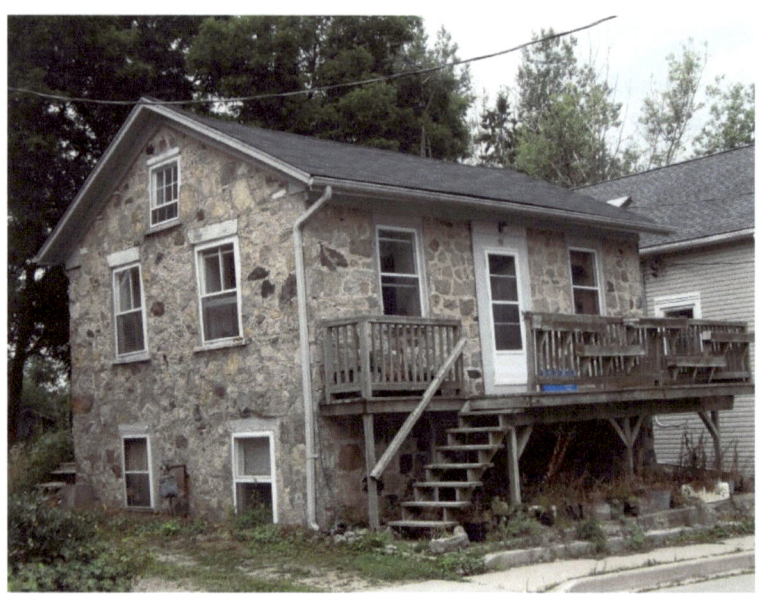

Gothic Revival - stone architecture

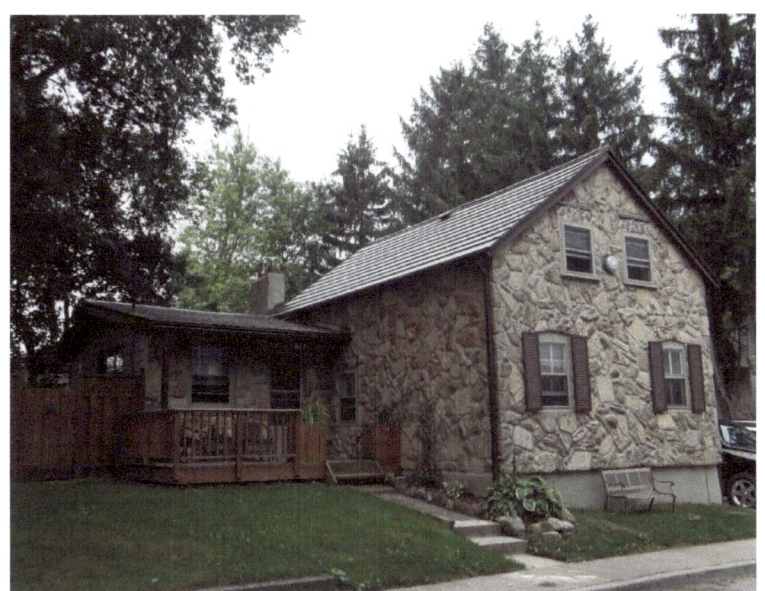

Gothic Revival - stone architecture

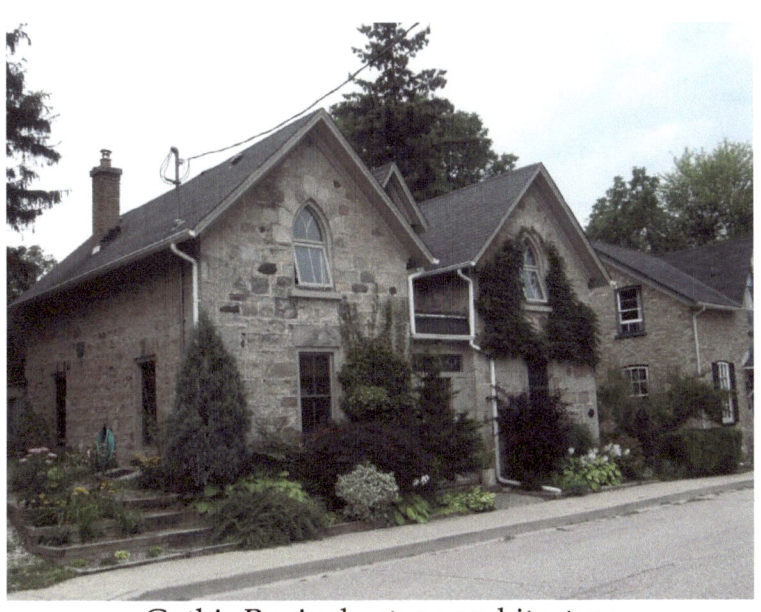

Gothic Revival - stone architecture

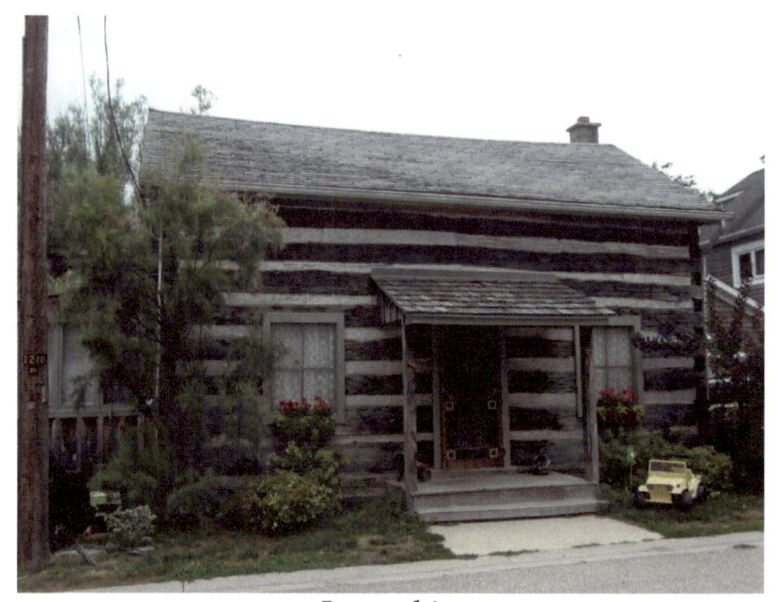

Log cabin

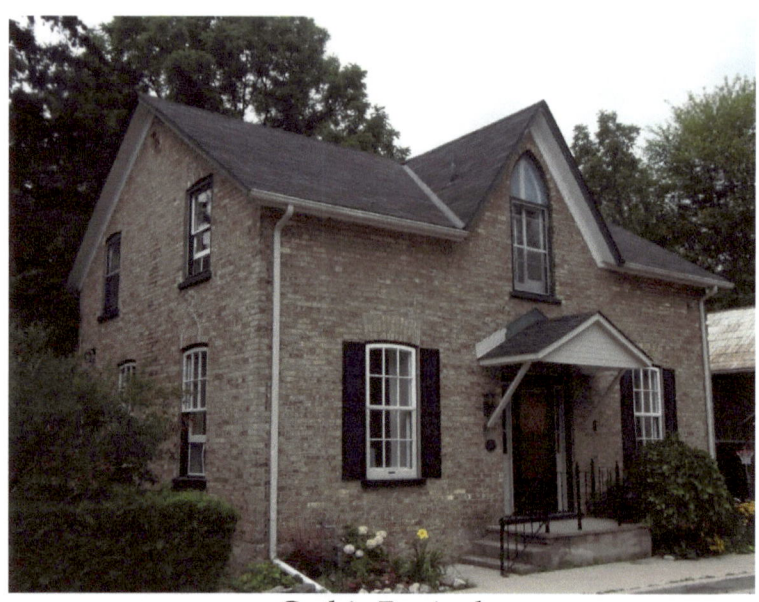

Gothic Revival

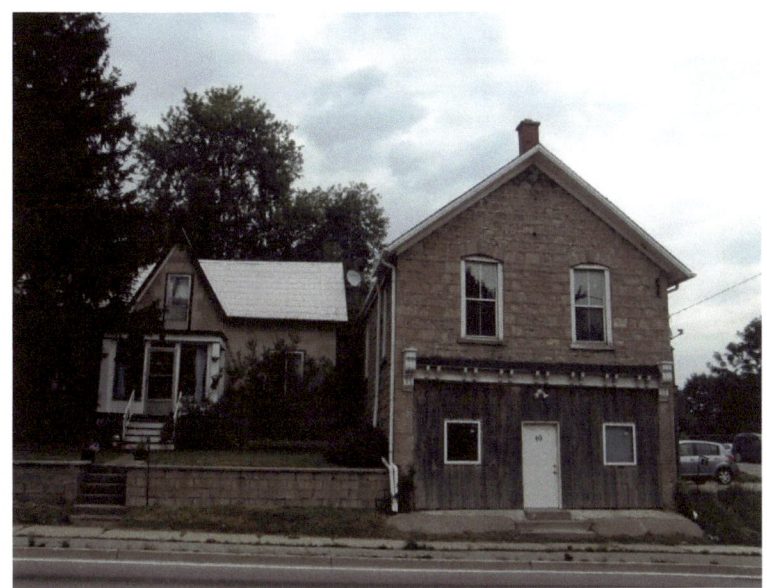

Gothic Revival - limestone

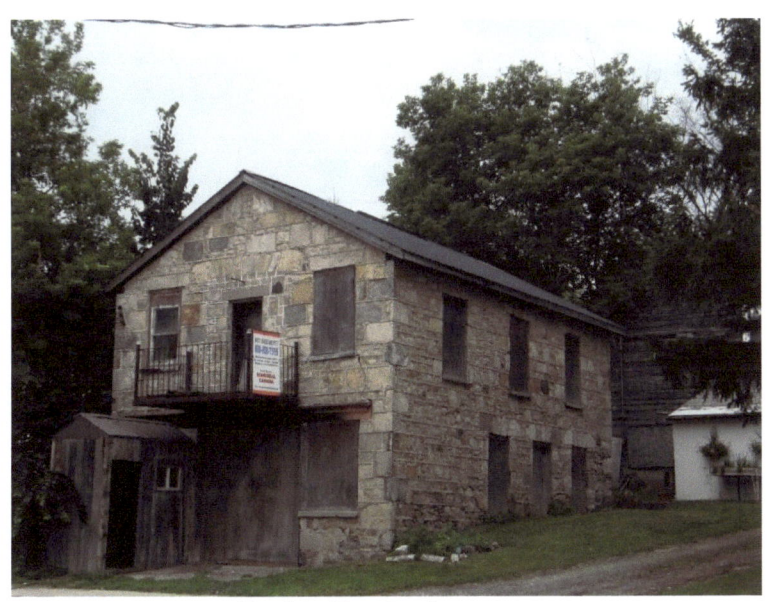

Gothic Revival – stone

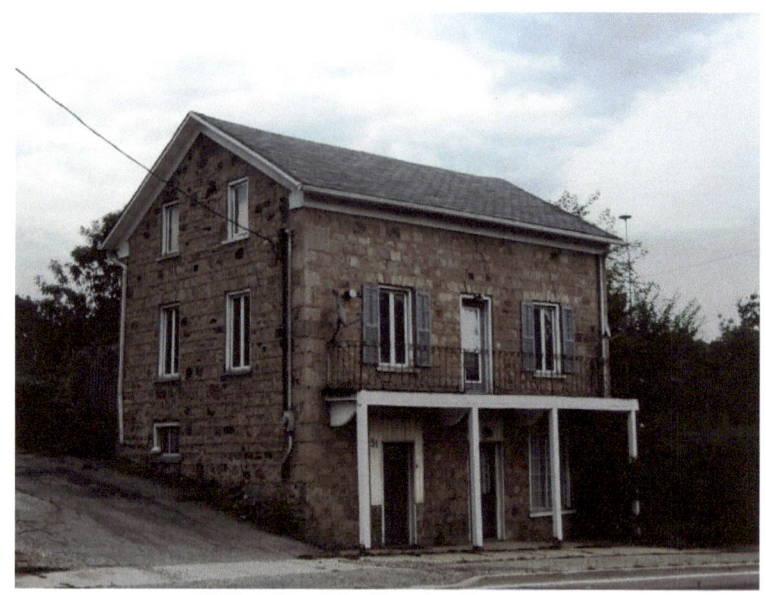

#51 - Gothic Revival – stone

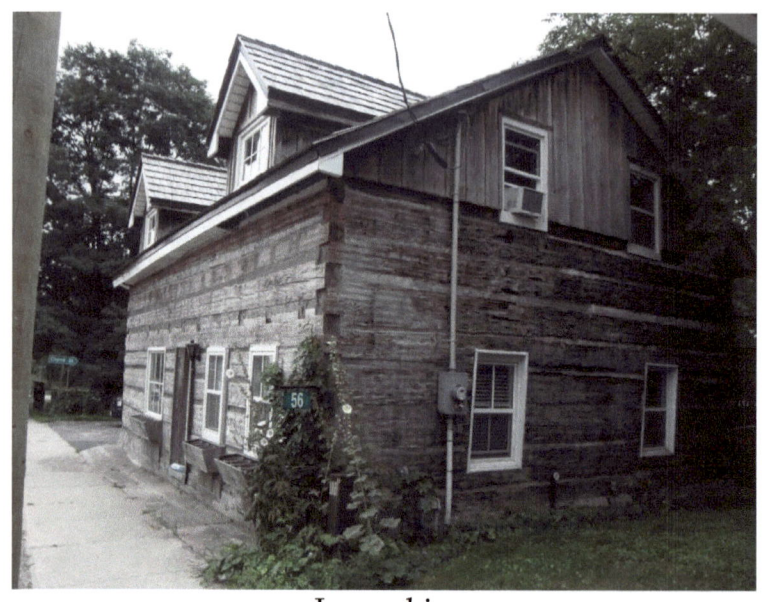

Log cabin

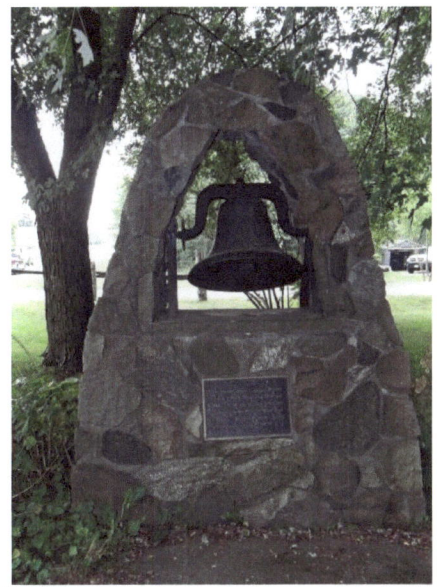

This bell called scholars to classes in Morriston School S.S. No. 8 Puslinch from 1910 to 1968. At that time the school district was consolidated under the Wellington County Board of Education and the school was closed.

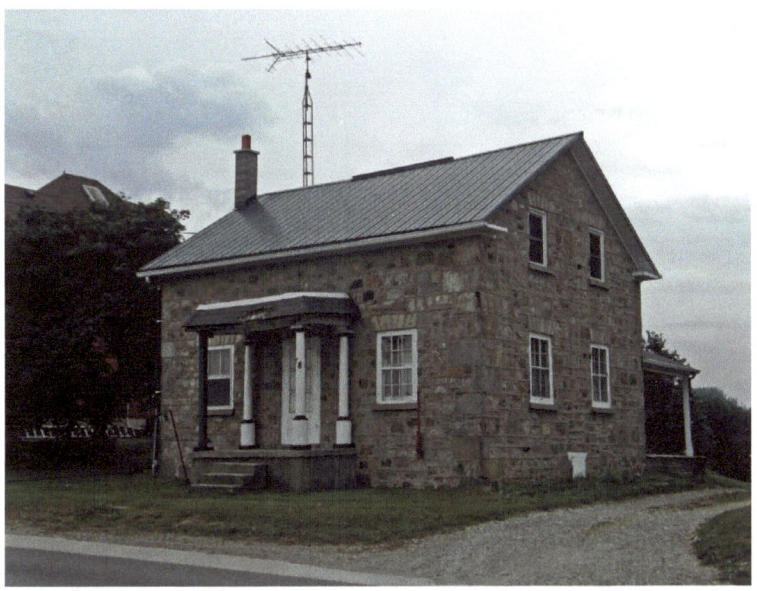

Gothic Revival –stone – cornice return on side gable

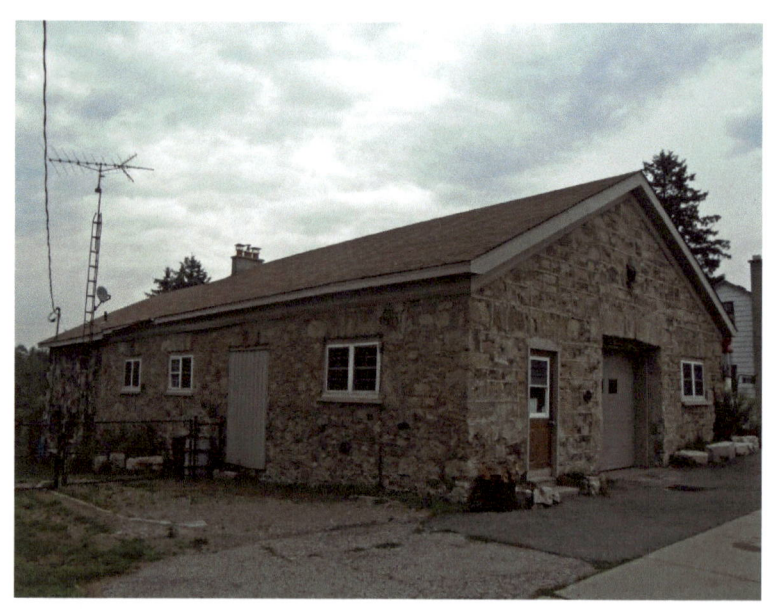

Puslinch Heritage Building – Gothic – stone

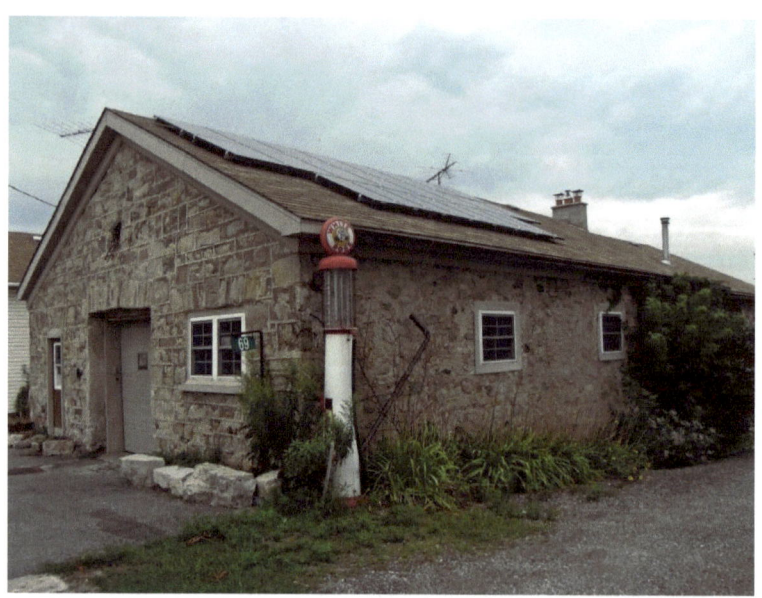

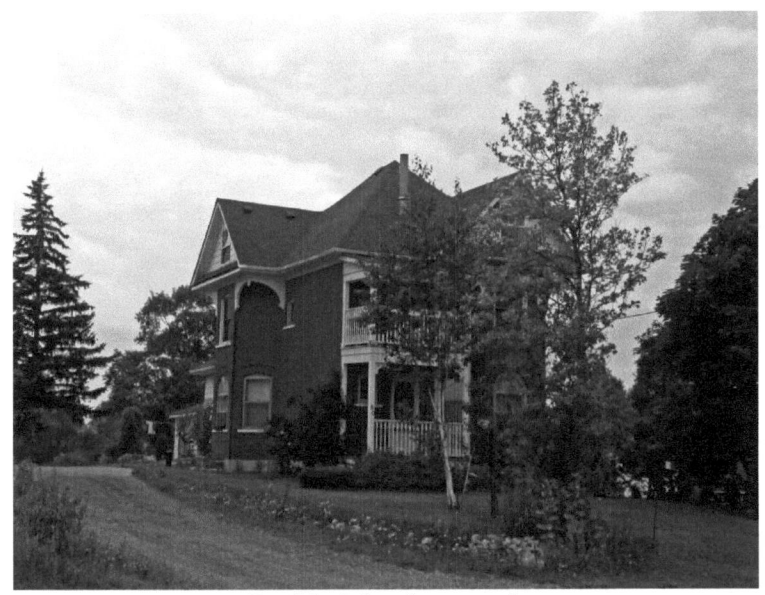
Red brick - fretwork

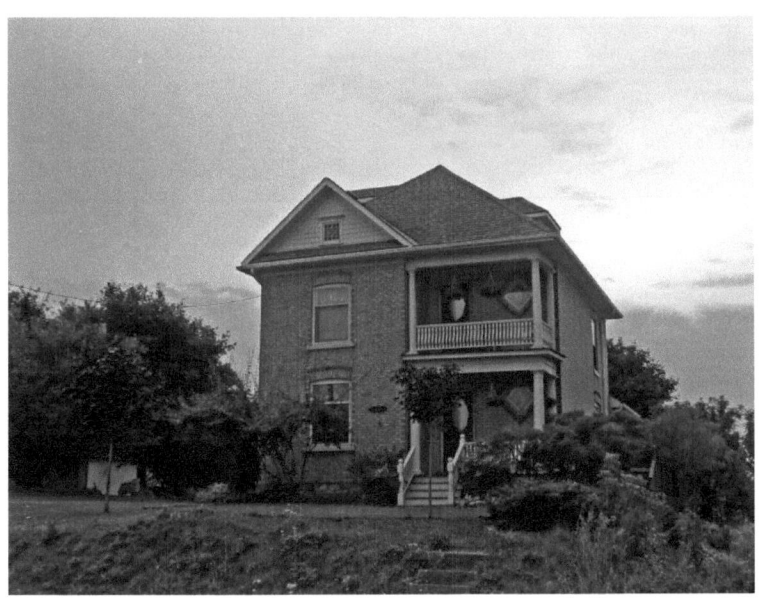
Yellow brick – balcony on second floor

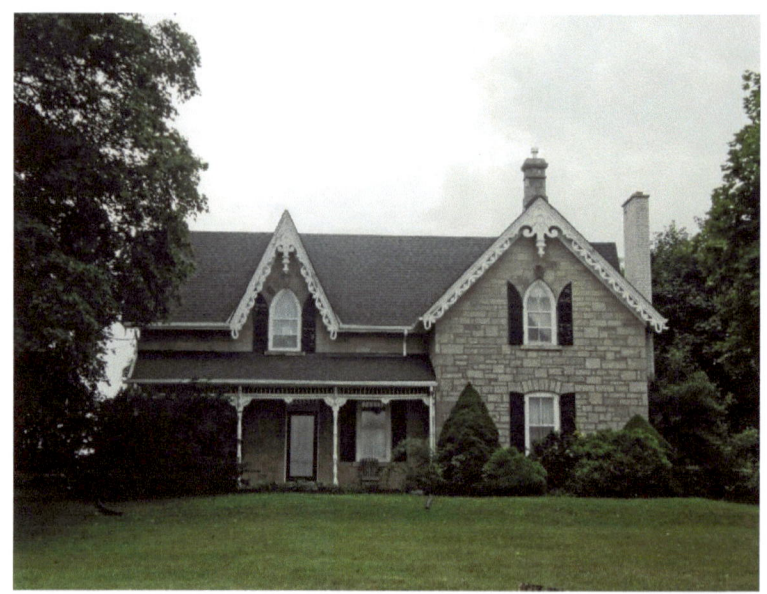

Gothic Revival – verge board trim on gables with finials

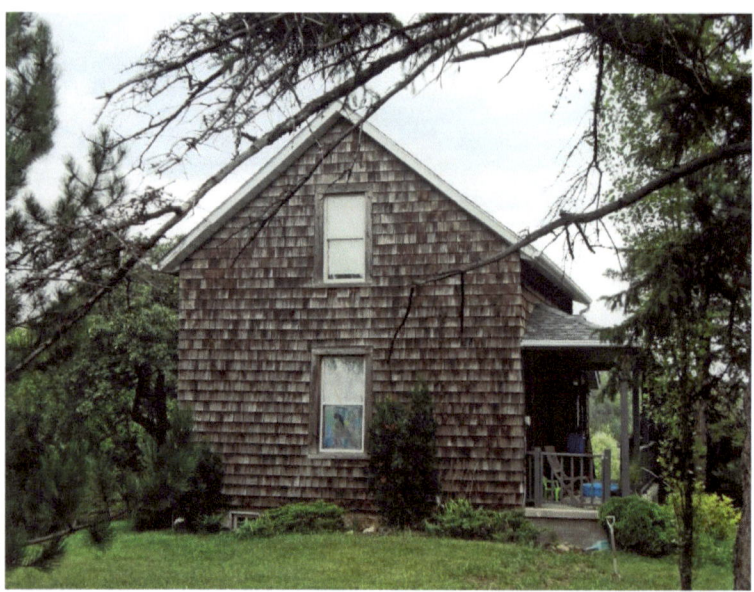

Cedar shake

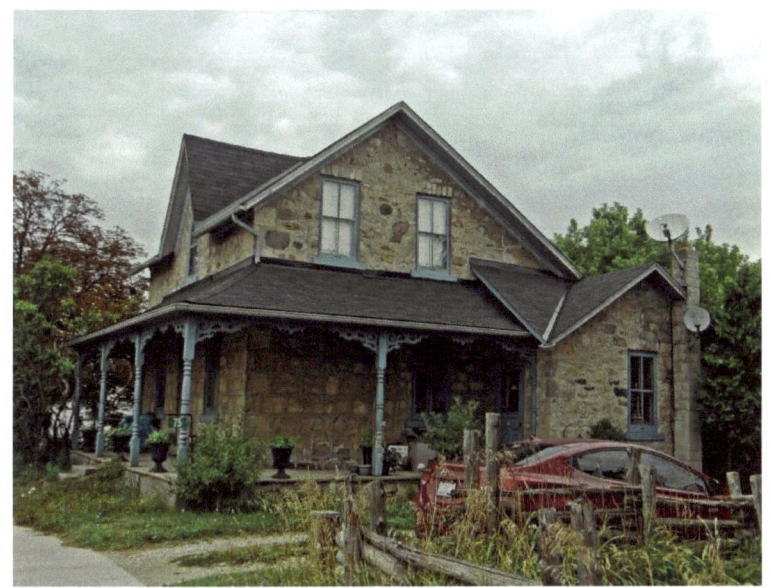

Gothic Revival – stone architecture

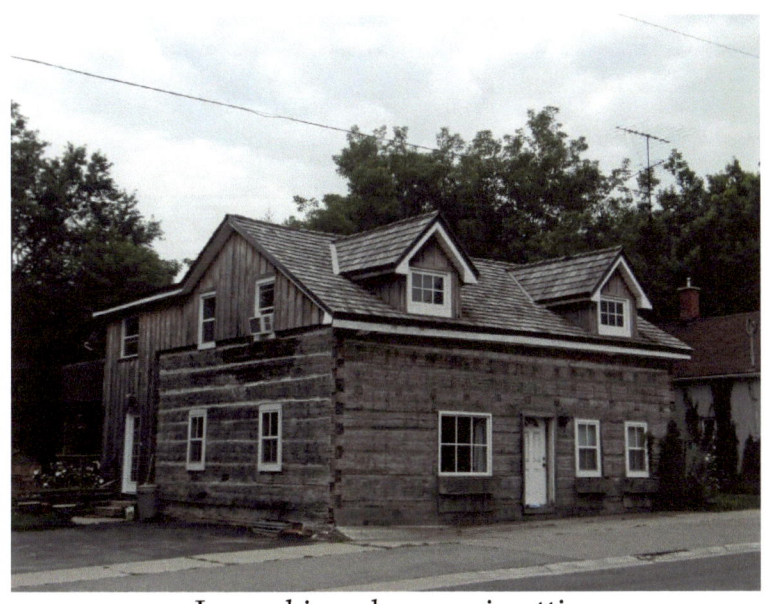

Log cabin – dormers in attic

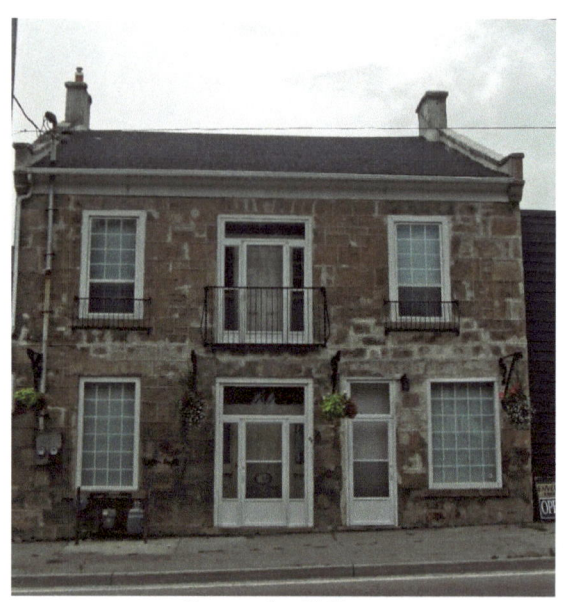

Stone building

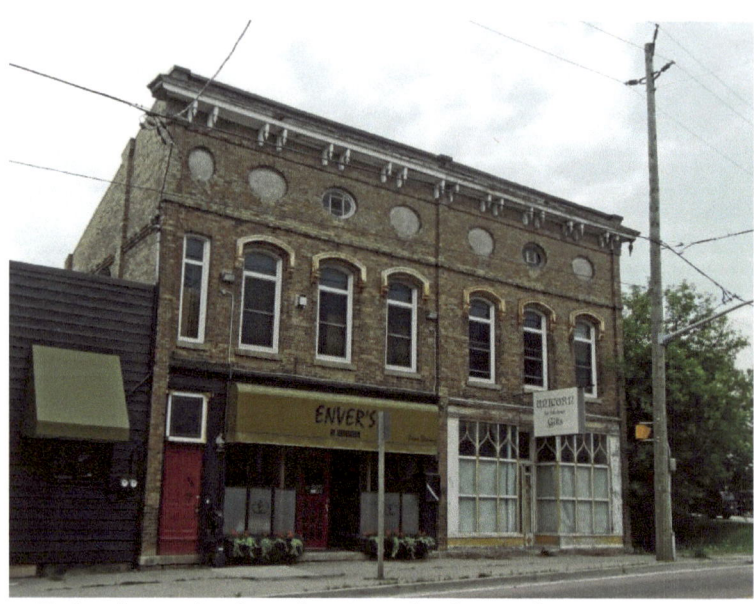

Paired cornice brackets, arched window voussoirs

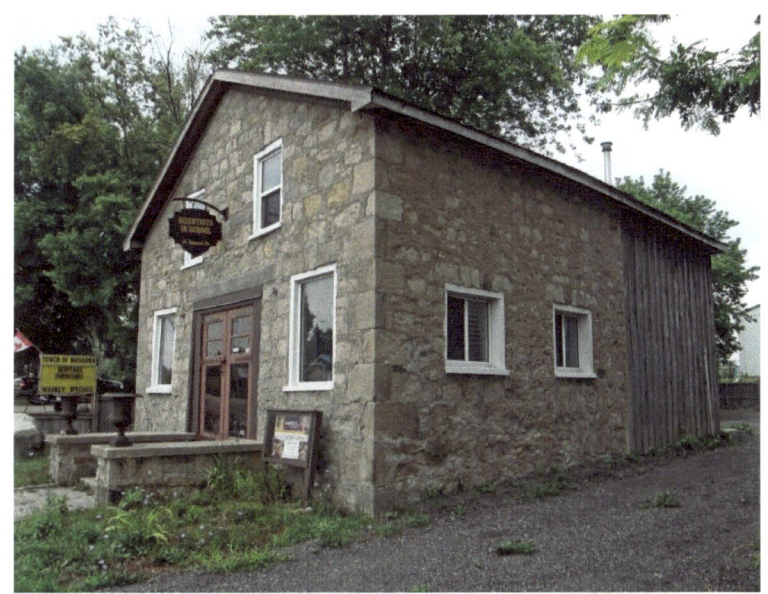

Gothic Revival –stone architecture

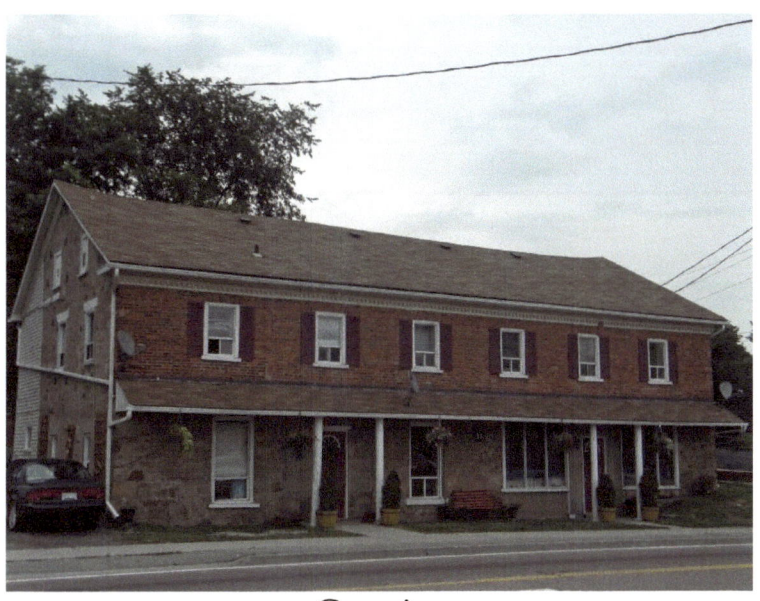

Georgian

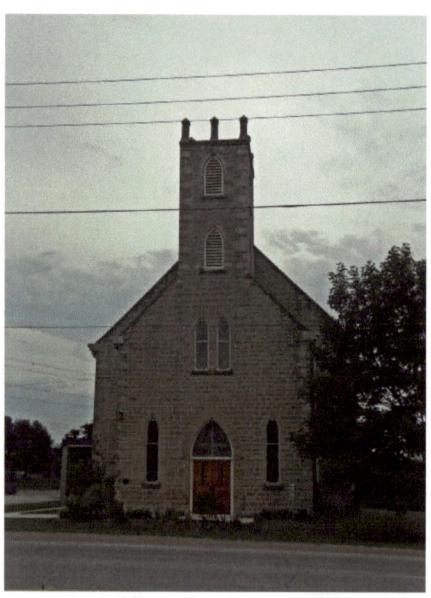

Duff's Church - 1903

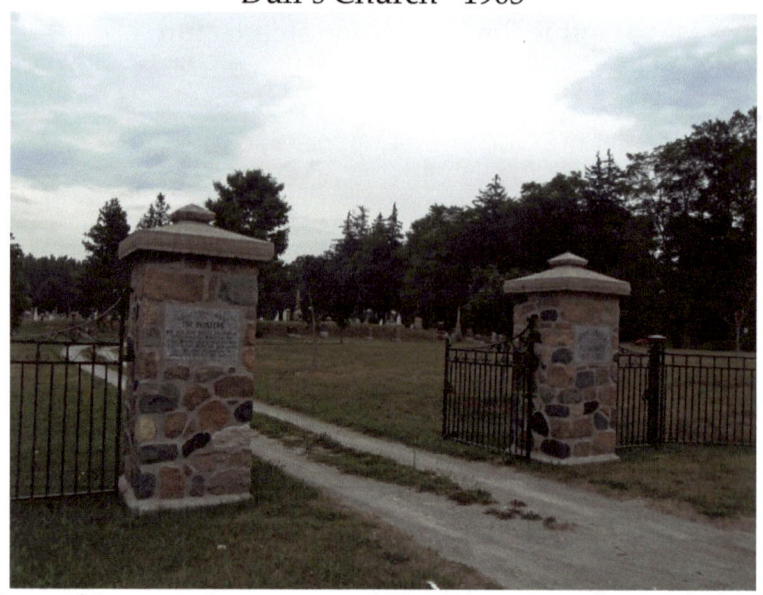

Erected in sacred memory of The Pioneers who with faith, courage and devotion established their homes and the public worship of God and also prepared a lasting resting place for their loved ones.

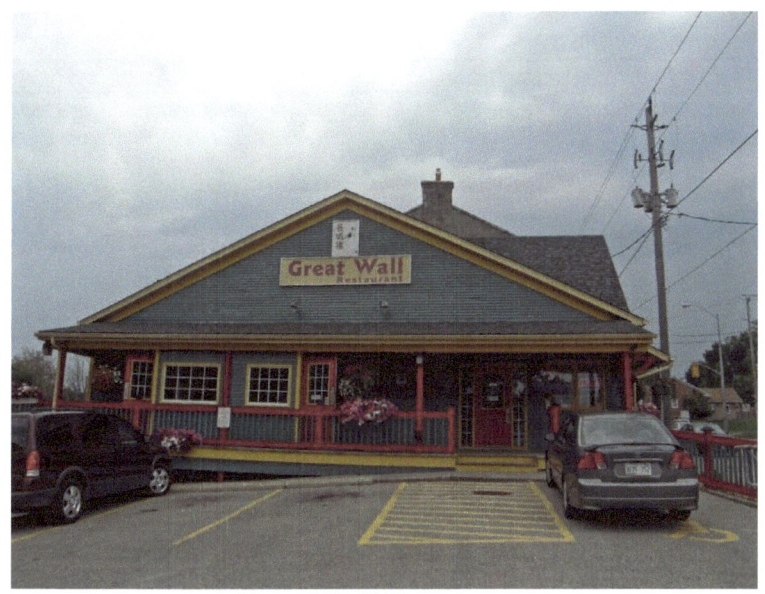

Great Wall Restaurant

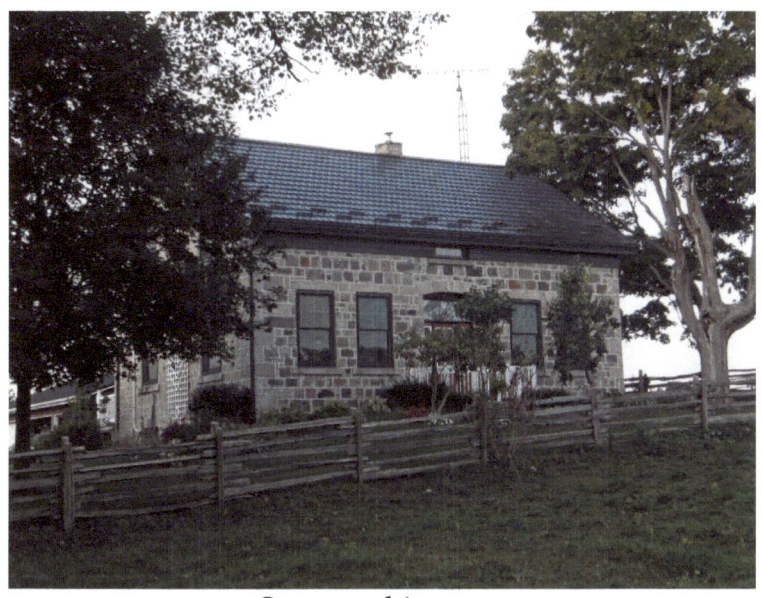

Stone architecture

Rockton

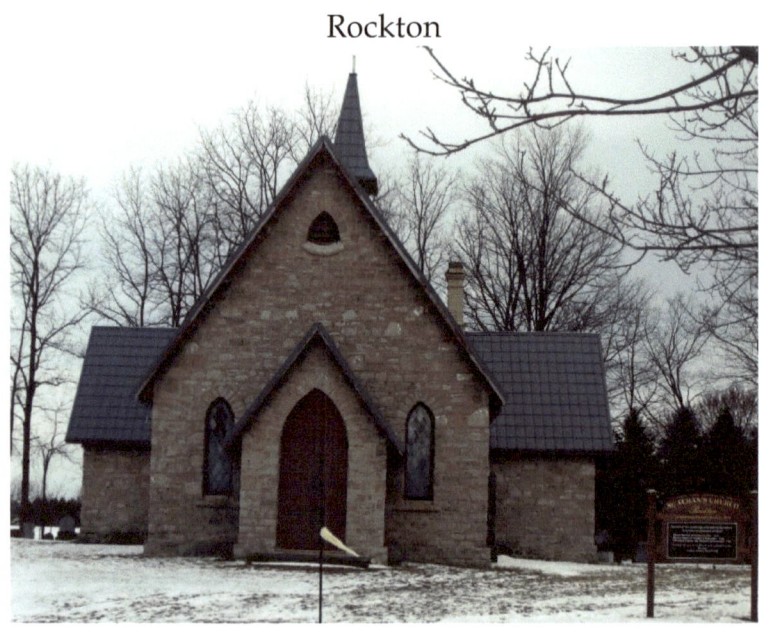

St. Alban's Church built in 1869
Gothic Revival, lancet windows

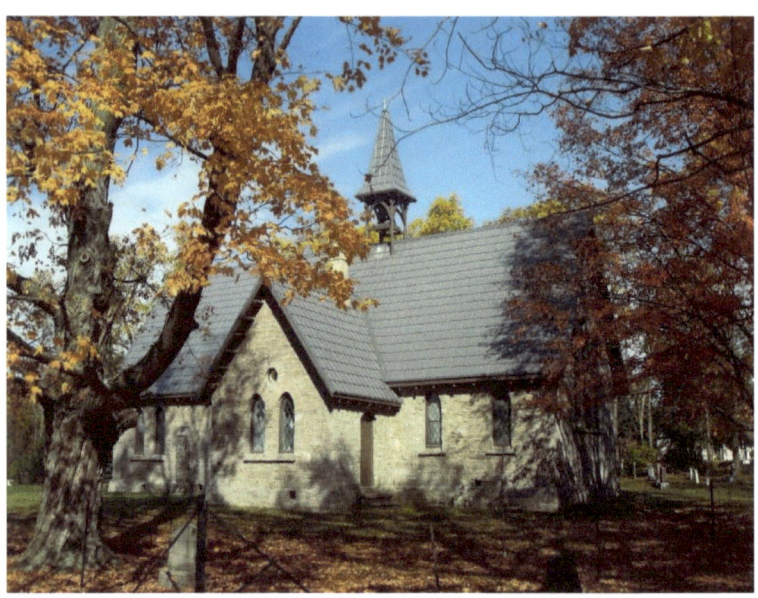

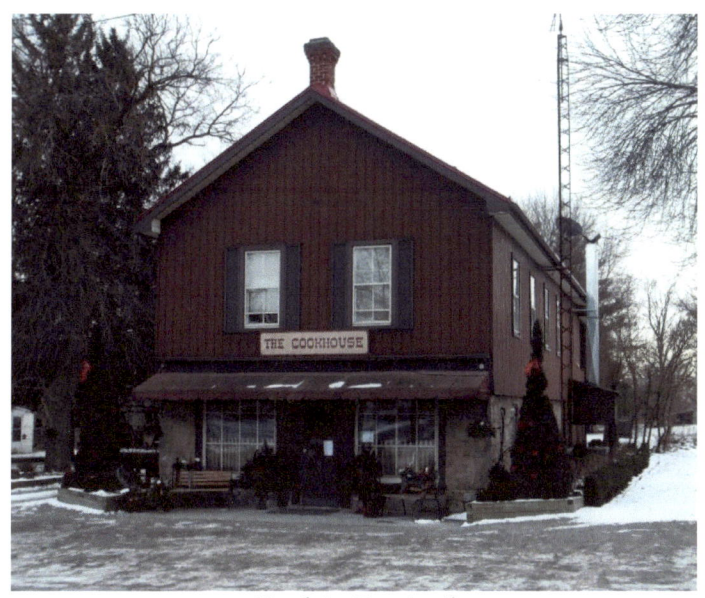

Gothic Revival

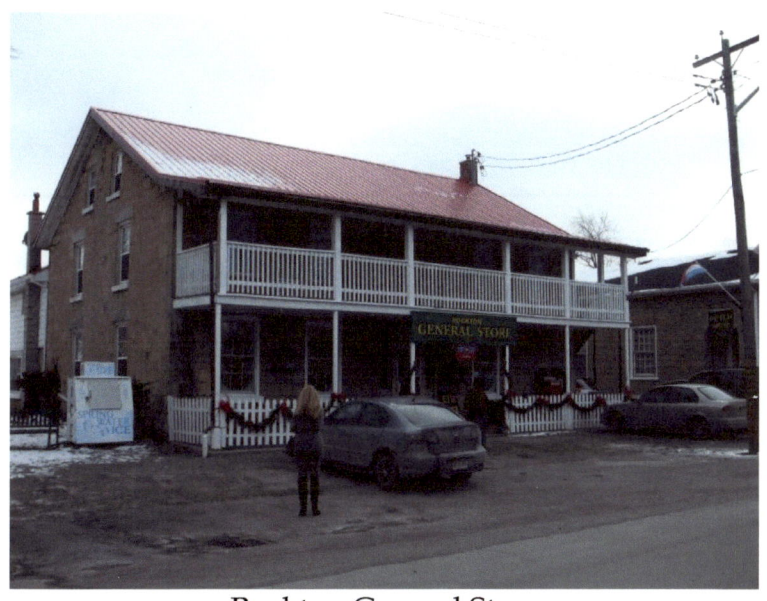

Rockton General Store

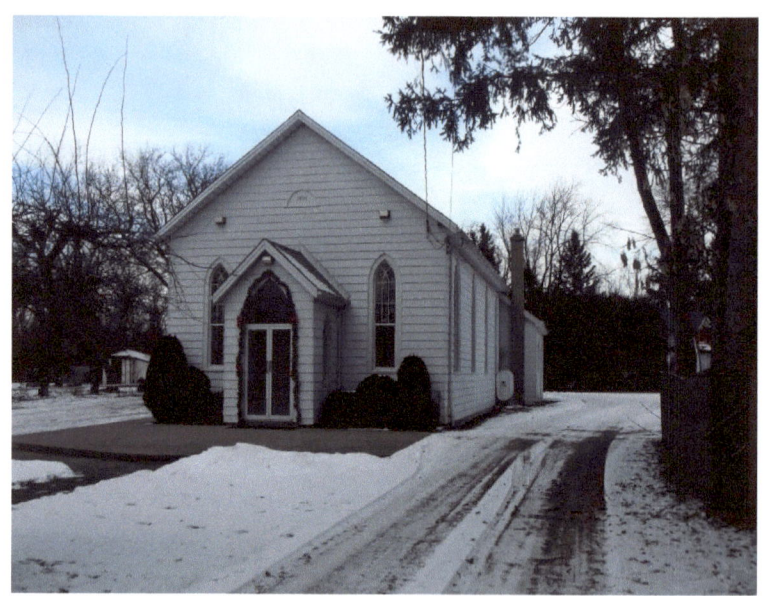

Rockton United Church - Gothic Revival

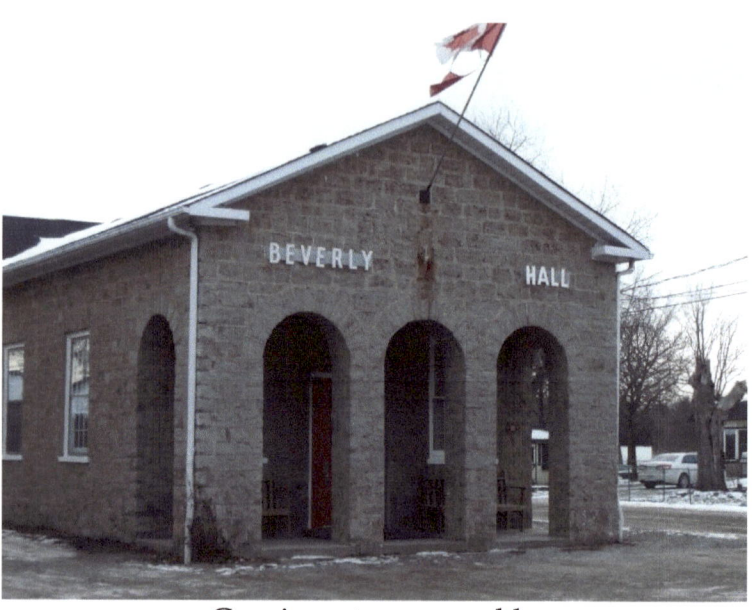

Cornice return on gable

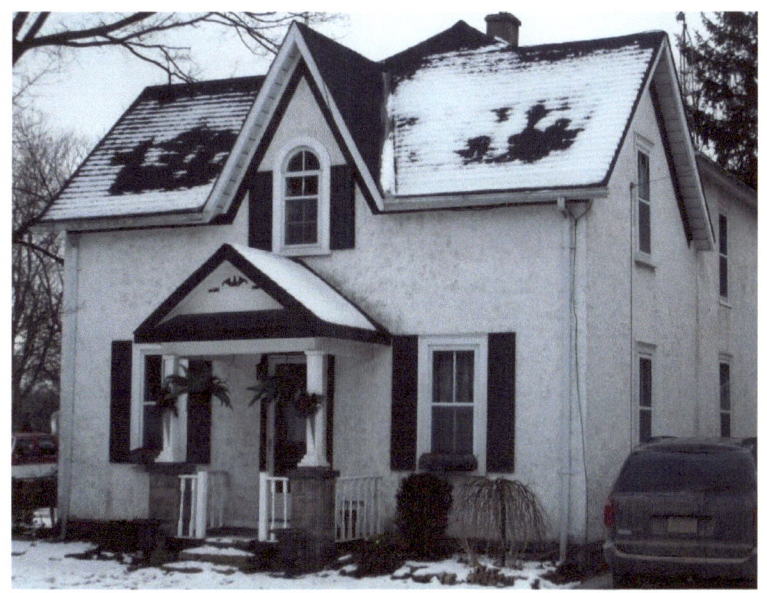

Gothic Revival – pediment above entranceway

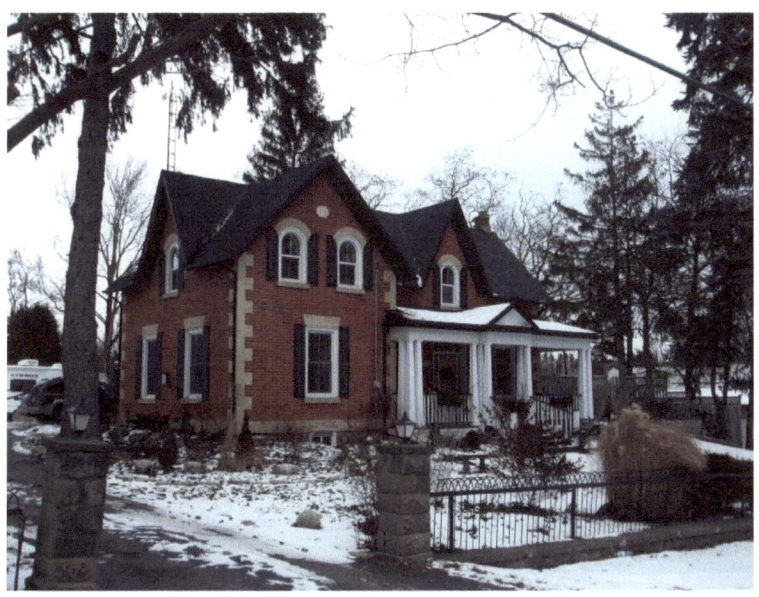

Gothic Revival – corner quoins

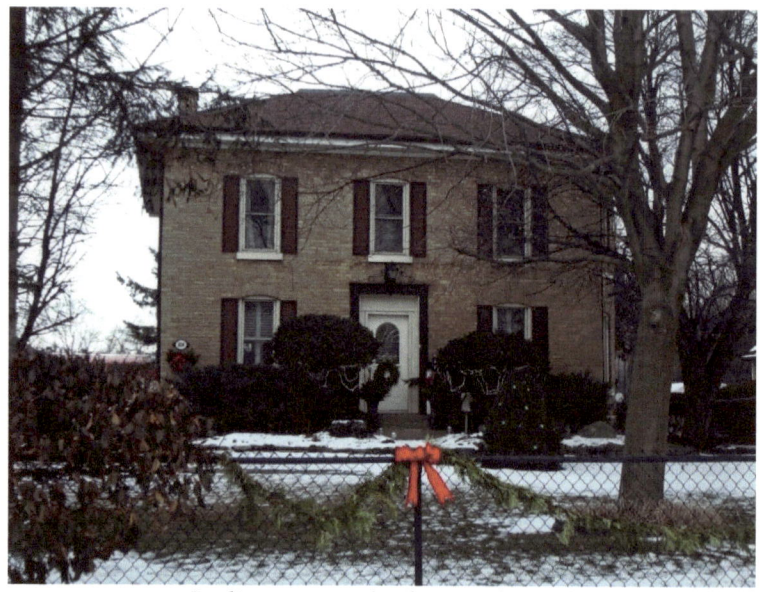

Italianate style, hipped roof

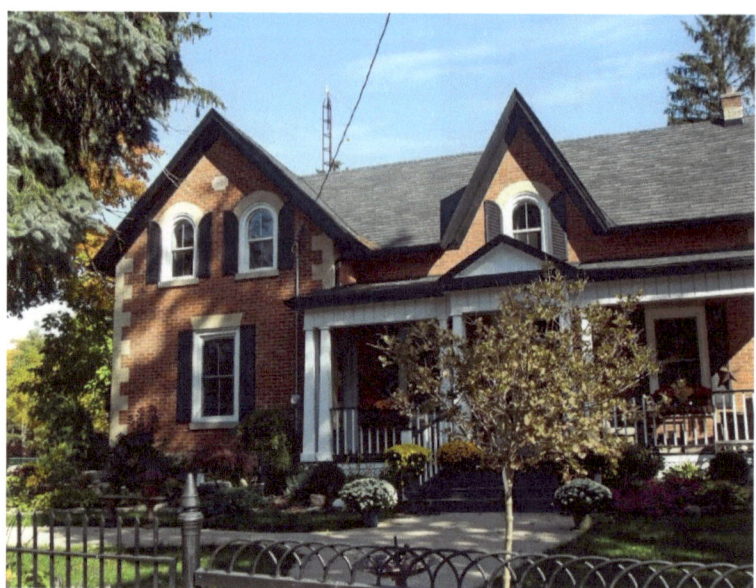

Gothic Revival, corner quoins

Architectural Terms

Brackets: a decorative or weight-bearing structural element which forms a right angle with one side against a wall and the other under a projecting surface such as an eave or roof. Example: Morriston	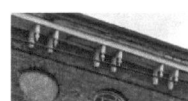
Cornice: originally the wooden overhang of the roof. With the use of stone, brick, iron and steel, the cornice is any projecting shelf at the top of a ceiling or roof. They can be very decorative. Example: Morriston	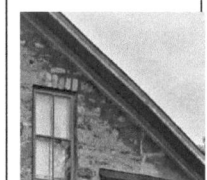
Cornice Return: decorative element on the end of a gable. Example: Morriston	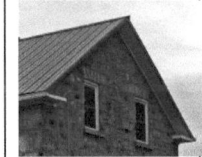
Dormer: (French for "sleep") a gable end window that pierces through the plane of a sloping roof surface to create usable space in the top floor or attic of a building by adding headroom. Example: Log cabin in Morriston	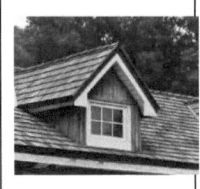

Finial: ornament added to the top of a gable, pinnacle, canopy or spire – a Gothic element. Example: Morriston	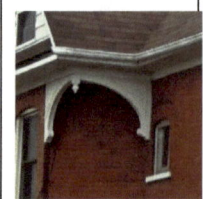
Fretwork: interlaced decorative design resembling a bracket Example: Morriston	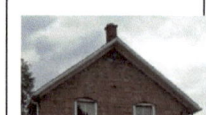
Gable: the triangular portion of a wall between the edges of a sloping roof. Example: Morriston	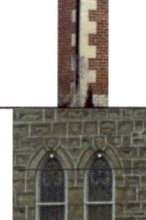
Quoin: masonry blocks at the corner of a wall, often a decorative feature, usually larger or of a different colour than the rest of the wall. Example: Rockton	
Lancet Window: a tall, narrow window with a pointed arch at its top. Example: Duff's Church	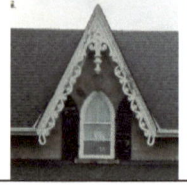
Verge boards: also called bargeboards – hang from the projecting end of a roof and are often elaborately carved and ornamented. Example: Morriston	

Aberfoyle, Morriston and Rockton's Building Styles

Georgian, before 1860 – This style began with the British King Georges in the 18th century. These buildings have balanced facades around a central door, medium-pitched gable roofs, and small paned windows. Example: Morriston	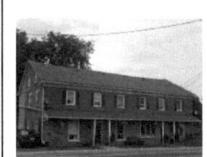
Gothic Revival, 1830-1890 – These decorative buildings have sharply-pitched gables with highly detailed verge boards, pointed-arch window openings, and dichromatic brickwork. It is a common style in Ontario. Example: Morriston	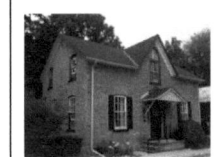
Italianate, 1850-1900 – It has wide-bracketed eaves, belvederes, wrap-around verandahs. Example: Rockton	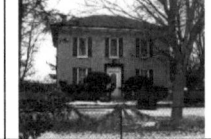
A log cabin, built from logs, was usually one- or 1½-storeys constructed with round rather than hewn, or hand-worked, logs, and erected quickly for frontier shelter. Log cabins were built from logs laid horizontally and interlocked on the ends with notches. The cabin was situated to provide sunlight and drainage so the pioneers could cope better with the rigors of frontier life. The pioneers chose old-growth trees that were straight and had few knots and did not need to be hewn to fit well together. Careful notching minimized the size of the gap between the logs and reduced the amount of chinking with sticks and rocks or daubing with mud to fill the gap. The length of one log was the length of one wall.	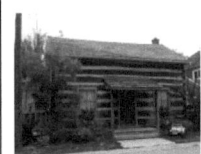